AUBREY BUR

PREHISTORIC HENGES

SHIRE ARCHAEOLOGY

Cover photographs
(Clockwise from top left)
Arbor Low, Derbyshire, a circle-henge (photograph: Aubrey Burl).
Gorsey Bigbury, Somerset (photograph: Jim Hancock).
The Giant's Ring, Ballynahatty, County Down
(photograph: Barrie Hartwell, Department of Archaeology,
School of Geosciences, The Queen's University of Belfast).

British Library Cataloguing in Publication Data:
Burl, Aubrey.
Prehistoric henges. — (Shire archaeology, 66).
1. Great Britain. Prehistoric antiquities.
I. Title.
936.101.
ISBN 0-7478-0123-1

*We are not agreed that all these monuments are of about the same age
and are ceremonial sites, that is to say 'temples' or 'meeting places'.*
T. D. Kendrick, 1932.

Published in 1997 by
SHIRE PUBLICATIONS LTD
Cromwell House, Church Street, Princes Risborough,
Buckinghamshire HP27 9AA, UK.

Series Editor: James Dyer.

ISBN 0 7478 0123 1

First published 1991; reprinted 1997.

Printed in Great Britain by
CIT Printing Services,
Press Buildings, Merlins Bridge, Haverfordwest, Pembrokeshire SA61 1XF.

Contents

List of illustrations

Note on dates

The radiocarbon or carbon-14 method of obtaining 'dates' from ancient organic material is misleading. Comparison with objects which can be historically dated, such as wooden articles from ancient Egypt, has shown that the carbon-14 results are too young and need to be extended backwards.

Through the counting of annual growth-rings in long-lived trees such as the bristlecone pines of the White Mountains of California, a procedure which gives the true age of any ring, and then subjecting the wood to radiocarbon analysis it has been possible to estimate the amount of error in the radiocarbon 'date'. From this calibration tables have been constructed which convert carbon-14 determinations into real years. A convenient reference is the table by Pearson *et al.* in *Radiocarbon* 28, 1986, 911-34.

It has become an archaeological convention to follow converted dates by BC, and unconverted carbon-14 determinations by bc. It is this system that is used here. Astronomical dates, based on the movements of heavenly bodies, are chronologically correct and therefore followed by BC.

Radiocarbon determinations are always followed by ±, indicating that there is a 2:1 chance that the object analysed 'died' between those years. Hence a 'date' for bone in the ditch at Stenness, Orkney, quoted at 2356±65 bc means that the chances are 2:1 in favour of the animal having died between 2421 bc and 2291 bc. This would be approximately 3130 BC to 2960 BC with a midpoint near to 3045 BC.

Acknowledgements

I would like to thank the following for their help and information: Gordon Barclay; Professor Richard Bradley; Jim Hancock; Professor Anthony Harding; Dr Roy Loveday; Dr Graham Ritchie; Ian Shepherd; Professor Derek Simpson; Geraldine Stout; and especial thanks to Peter Saunders, Curator of Salisbury and South Wiltshire Museum, for allowing me to show how the antler picks and sarsen mauls were used in the construction of Stonehenge.

1
Introduction

'**Henge**. A type of ritual monument found only in the British Isles and consisting of a circular area, anything from 150 to 1700 feet [46 to 518 metres] across, delimited by a ditch with the bank normally *outside* it.'
W. Bray and D. Trump, *A Dictionary of Archaeology* (1970), 103.

Henges are strange places. To the casual eye they seem dull, no more than a circular bank of earth and rubble surrounding a turf-covered interior. There is nothing else to see. Yet henges were places vitally needed by their builders, places for gatherings at the great times of the year, places where sacred objects were ritually buried, places of the sun and moon, of the axe, perhaps even of sacrifices.

They were the earthen counterparts of the stone circles in the west of Great Britain and Ireland. But whereas many of those rings remain spectacular, their stones stark on the hillsides and moors, henges have been eroded and smoothed down by wind, rain and storm. Built on soft earths, gravels and chalk, their banks have weathered away, their ditches have collapsed and filled, and grass has spread over the worn-down outlines of those once mountainous earthworks.

Originally they were spacious and outstanding, the centres of great assemblies in summer and winter. Today they are quiet, almost neglected. Many of them have been ploughed and levelled, their traces only visible from aerial photographs (figure 1). Not surprisingly, people have preferred to go to stone circles, where the ring can be seen plainly and where the visitor's imagination can enliven the silence with visions of rites that were last performed there more than four thousand years ago. It is an irony that henges have provided much greater knowledge of what those rites were.

1.5 km (1 mile) north-east of Cheddar Gorge in Somerset, on private land near a stream, there is a grassy ring. Low, often overgrown with bracken, and capable of being strolled across in less than a minute, it is easily overlooked. So is the irregular space that its bank surrounds. Yet the name, Gorsey Bigbury, suggests that this had been an impressive enclosure, 'the gorse-covered great earthwork'.

It is one of nearly one hundred henges in Britain and Ireland, dating from about 3200 BC. These enclosures had banks that often were composed of material dug from an inner ditch. One or more gaps through the bank and uninterrupted causeways across the ditch provided entrances to a central plateau where meetings and ceremonies were held, some of them strange to the modern mind. Even the word 'henge'

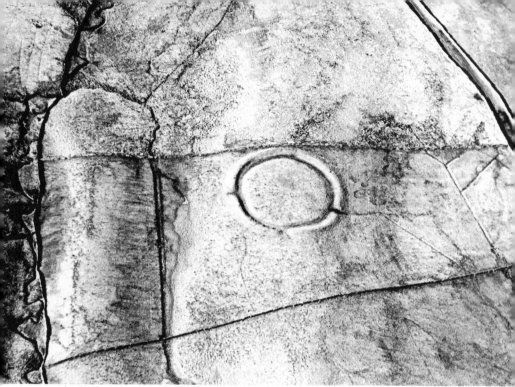

1. Castle Dykes, North Yorkshire, from the air. The inner ditch and the two entrances are visible. Field walls enclose the earthwork. (Photograph: D. Riley.)

is strange and misleading. It comes from the Old English *stanhengen* or 'hanging stones', the ancient name for Stonehenge, inside whose circle five gigantic pairs of uprights have lintels across their tops like the structure of a medieval gallows. It is paradoxical that Gorsey Bigbury and most other 'henges' never contained stones either singly or on top of one another.

The bank at Gorsey Bigbury (figure 2) was deliberately reduced and spread out by landowners in the eighteenth and nineteenth centuries so that to the uninformed viewer it is an unexciting place. Yet excavations between 1931 and 1934 and in 1965 recovered evidence of massive labour, of interest in the sun, of practices tantamount to witchcraft, of abandonment and then reoccupation by people with beliefs different from those of the henge builders.

In the beginning a ditch was quarried out of the hard limestone on which the henge was to stand (figure 3). 1500 tonnes of rubble were prised, wedged and dragged from the trench, which was dug in five untidy segments with perhaps ten workers in each. With a narrow space left between the ditch's outer lip and the inner edge of the bank, the bits and lumps of broken stone were dumped to form a wide but low bank. To heighten this, the labourers dug out tonnes of soil from the

central area, lowering it, heaping basketloads of earth over the limestone debris of the bank, raising it to head height.

An entrance four long strides across was left at almost the exact north.
Similar north-south alignments occur at the nearby henges of Priddy 6
km (4 miles) to the east-southeast and at the Hunter's Lodge henge 10
km (6 miles) away. In the centuries before magnetic compasses, and
with no Pole Star to help them, observers must have watched the risings
and settings of some celestial object, probably the sun, and bisected
them to establish these cardinal points.

Two slight posts were set up at the entrance as portals, held firmly in
their holes with pieces not of local stone but of red sandstone, 'definite
evidence of selection by men', according to the excavator. An interest
in colours, textures and minerals on the part of prehistoric people has
been noticed at other henges, including Stonehenge.

The construction of such a heavy earthwork must have demanded
months of toil by the able-bodied of the community. Yet not many

2. Plan of Gorsey Bigbury henge, Somerset. (Drawing: A. Burl.)

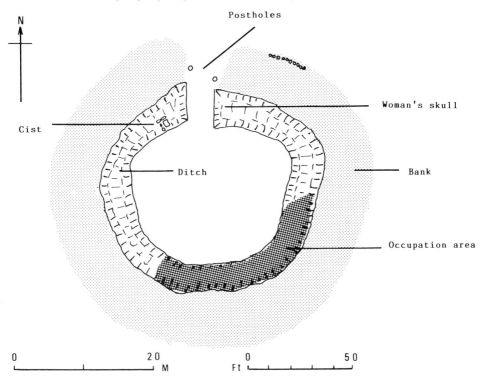

years after it was finished the henge was abandoned, its builders perhaps driven away by newcomers who were to have another use for it.
Within years the edges of the ditch crumbled. Leaves and soil dropped
and drifted on to its bottom, sifting against the limestone slabs of a cist,
a stone-lined grave, near the western side of the entrance. Three corpses
had been buried there, a man, a young woman and a five-year old child.
Theirs was no ordinary funeral. They may even have been a family

3. The rock-cut ditch at Stenness, Orkney. 620 cubic metres (1270 tonnes) of sandstone
were quarried from it. The work demanded 12,500 man-hours of labour. (Photograph:
G. Ritchie.)

sacrificed to bring power to the henge. Months later, when the bodies were skeletal, the cist was opened and most of the bones were bundled out and flung with complete indifference on to the untidy litter of the ditch. Only the man's skull and a few longer bones were left untouched, with some tools, bone pins, a flint knife and arrowhead and a sherd of a decorated beaker.

The man's other bones and those of the woman and the child were thrown out. One of the man's powerful forearms had been broken and reset. 'The repair was so perfect that it is doubtful if it could have been done better.' Near it lay broken fragments of the child's skull, maybe deliberately smashed to 'kill' it. With them were the woman's scattered bones, including her jawbone but not her skull, which was found near the entrance. It lay in a pit newly dug down into the ditch alongside the eastern edge of the causeway. The skull had been carefully deposited as though to protect the henge. Similar 'guardian' burials of human beings have been found at the entrances of other henges such as Stonehenge.

It has been thought that the builders of Gorsey Bigbury, families using pottery known as Grooved Ware, whose flat-bottomed vessels have often been found in henges, had been expelled by a group preferring the more elaborate beaker pots. Whoever they were, their occupation of the site was not a reverent one. Broken vessels, bones, cut for their meat, of pig, cattle and sheep, flint knives, awls, scrapers, flakes for their manufacture, human refuse, all were cast into the southern half of the ditch, which was turned into an unwholesome midden. Charcoal showed where fires had destroyed some of the rubbish. Radiocarbon determinations from the organic remains, from as early as 1850±74 bc down to 1652±71 bc, proved that the occupation, unlike that of the first people, had been an extended one, about 250 years from 2300 to 2050 BC.

Lumps of burnt daub from the far side of the henge hinted at the former existence of a flimsy timber dwelling, lath-panelled and wattled. The impression was of settlers grazing cattle, keeping pigs and sheep, occasionally hunting, growing barley on the rich brown earths of the area, hand-making fine pottery, and using the henge as a useful dump and windbreak for some generations before they too moved away, leaving the earthwork slowly to mellow back into the landscape.

People had built it. People abused it. It is the people who constructed such great enclosures who provide most of the clues about the purpose of henges. But there was little uniformity. These earthworks were built in regions hundreds of miles apart. In each region their construction differed. There was no international blueprint for the design of a henge in Britain and Ireland.

Prehistoric Henges

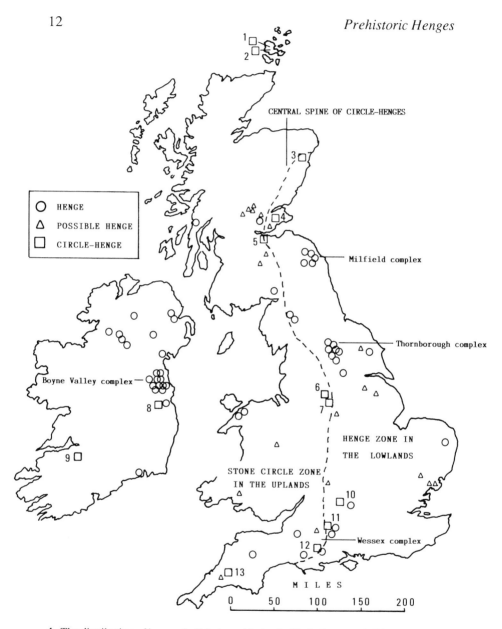

4. The distribution of henges in Britain and Ireland. Circle-henges: 1, Ring of Brodgar; 2, Stones of Stenness; 3, Broomend of Crichie; 4, Balfarg; 5, Cairnpapple; 6, Bull Ring; 7, Arbor Low; 8, Castleruddery; 9, Grange (Lios); 10, Devil's Quoits; 11, Avebury; 12, Stonehenge; 13, Stripple Stones. (Drawing: A. Burl.)

2
Henges

Henges have been defined as roughly circular earthworks with a bank surrounding an inner ditch and broken by one or more entrances. Like most brief definitions, however, the description is accurate but inadequate, omitting the variety of kinds and sizes within the species. There are many types of henge.

They can be divided into two main groups. Class I henges have a single entrance, Class II more than one although rarely more than two. There are subdivisions. Class I and II henges do have only a single internal ditch but Class IA and IIA sites, such as the Thornborough henges in North Yorkshire, have two ditches, one on either side of the bank. Class IB and IIB henges have a single ditch but one which is outside the bank. Class IC and IIC are henges without any ditch, many Irish henges being outstanding examples.

Table 1. Types of henge in Britain and Ireland.

Class	Feature	Distribution
I II	Single internal ditch	Widespread in Britain
IA IIA	Two ditches	Eastern England
IB IIB	Single external ditch	Very rare
IC IIC	No ditch	Western Britain, Ireland

The most common henges, those with a single inner ditch, occur in almost every henge area from the Orkneys down to Cornwall, from Yorkshire westwards to Ireland (figure 4). This is not true of the others. Despite some overlapping, the 'A', 'B' and 'C' henges occupy largely distinct regions in Britain and Ireland.

The double-ditched 'A' enclosures are to be found almost exclusively in eastern England from Arminghall (IA) in Norfolk to the concentration of IIA earthworks on the fertile plain between the Swale and Ure rivers in North Yorkshire. There are two western outliers on the fringes of Wessex, at Condicote (IA) in Gloucestershire and Dorchester Big Rings (IIA) in Oxfordshire.

The riverine Yorkshire sites are immense. Cana, Hutton Moor (figure 5) and all the three Thornborough henges that are set in a straight NNW-SSE line over 1.5 km (1 mile) in length are spacious, and so is the Class II Nunwick nearby. The central plateaux of these enclosures are remarkably similar in shape and size, slightly ovoid and varying no more than 5 metres or so from a norm of 97 by 92 metres. All have their entrances near the north-west and south-east following the lie of the land.

Each of them could have held as many as two thousand people and yet they crowd together in a narrow rectangle 11 km (7 miles) long and no more than 1.5 km (1 mile) across, like an avenue of architect-designed houses with a river frontage to their west.

Unlike the relatively numerous 'A' forms, the Type B henges, those with an outer ditch, are rare, no more than nine or ten being known. Most are quite close together in the west, the others at Stonehenge and at Priddy in Somerset being miles away in Wessex.

Llandegai North (IB) near Bangor, Gwynedd, with dates of 2470±140 bc (*c*.3200 BC) from ditch material, and 2530±145 bc (*c*.3350 BC) from a cremation outside its west entrance, may have been one of the very first henges to be erected.

5. Aerial view of Hutton Moor henge, North Yorkshire. The bank is the white ring. The inner and outer dark rings are the earth-filled ditches. (Photograph: © Crown copyright 1991/MOD. Reproduced with the permission of the Controller of HMSO.)

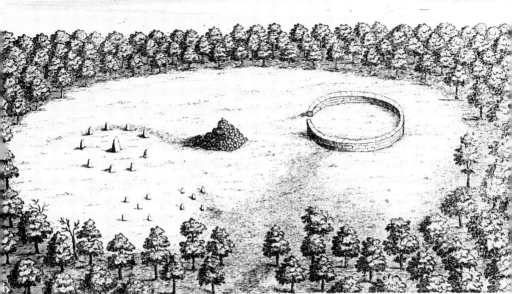

6. An eighteenth-century reconstruction of Castell Bryn-gwyn henge, Anglesey. A cairn and stone circles stand outside the west entrance. The henge was converted into an iron age fortification. (Collection of A. Burl.)

Just across the Menai Straits, on Anglesey, the henge of Castell Bryn-gwyn, 'the fortress of the white hill' (figure 6), whose stony bank was later remodelled for defence, also had a narrow entrance close to the west.

Directly across the Irish Sea, only 120 km (75 miles) from Anglesey and 26 km (16 miles) south-southeast of Dublin, is the banked perfect circle of Longstone Rath (IIB), its central area 60 metres across, with opposed entrances at west and east. Such consistent westerly orientations, coupled with their unusual outer ditches, suggest that the three earthworks do form a genuine group. Given their cardinal point alignments, it is interesting that Stonehenge (IIB) has its second entrance at the exact south (figure 7). Of the three at Priddy (IB), two have northern entrances, the third a gap at the south.

The final type of exotic henge, Type C, lacking a ditch and with a bank built of material scraped from the interior rather than from ditches or pits, has a nucleus in eastern Ireland, where three small groups cluster in a triangle of some 180 square kilometres between the Boyne, Nanny and Delvin rivers. It is noteworthy that all the other ditchless sites, Mayburgh (IC) near Penrith in Cumbria, henges such as Meinigwyr (IC) in south-west Wales, the Giant's Ring (IC or IIC?) near Belfast (front cover), even the Grange circle (IC) in County Limerick, lie in a ring 240 km (150 miles) in radius from the Boyne heartland.

Like the Type A sites, the unditched henges are large and generally oval in shape. Many of them have been severely ploughed down and their entrances destroyed but fieldwork and aerial photography have

7. The narrow causeway at the exact south of Stonehenge. Beyond is the lowest stone (number 11) of the later sarsen circle. (Photograph: A. Burl.)

provided evidence of enormous enclosures. The best preserved is the site known as Dowth Q (IIC), with an ovoid interior about 175 by 165 metres. The bank still stands up to 5 metres high and there are apparent entrances at the south-west and north-east. This is unusual. The majority of Type C henges have a broad east-west orientation, a trait shared by Meini-gwyr and Mayburgh.

Monknewton in County Meath is the only Irish example to be excavated. A date of 1860±45 bc (c.2350 BC) was obtained from charcoal in the remains of a scanty house within the enclosure.

There is an interesting juxtaposition of types near the confluence of the Eamont and Lowther rivers by modern Penrith. Here the heavy, stone-piled bank of Mayburgh (IC) at the gateway to the Lake District stands within a few hundred metres of the slighter henge of King Arthur's Round Table (II). A third henge, perhaps Type B, may have existed nearby at the now destroyed Little Round Table. The antiquarian William Stukeley, who saw it in 1725, wrote that 'the vallum (bank) is small, and the ditch whence it is taken is outermost'. That three such different earthworks should be so close together suggests they may have been the separate sanctuaries of strangers from distant parts where they could meet, perhaps trade, in safety. It seems significant that all three lay just outside the pass along which stone axes from the Langdale mountains were carried.

From the marked variation in henges it can be seen that there existed clear-cut regional types of henge and ones that are comparatively easy to categorise. Yet, perplexingly, Stonehenge, the very first henge to be so named, has persistently been wrongly classified. It is always said to belong to Class I, a henge with an inner ditch and a single entrance. It belongs, in fact, to Class II and subdivision B. It possesses not one but two entrances, one at the south and a wider one at the north-east, and it has an outer ditch. It also has two banks. In this it is almost unique. To add to the confusion, the stone circle for which Stonehenge is best known was added a full thousand years after the construction of the earthwork.

Henges varied regionally in age and size. Some were as early as 3200 BC but the great majority were built in the late neolithic and early bronze ages of Britain and Ireland for almost a millennium from about 2700 down to 2000 BC. The beginning of this period followed years of disturbance when many customs and ways of life had been disrupted. New cults appeared. One of them was associated with the poorly made pottery known as Grooved Ware whose origins are still obscure but whose users are believed to have been the builders of several early henges. Different and more elegant vessels, the beakers, perhaps brought into Britain by people from the European mainland, have also been recovered from henges during this late neolithic period.

The fact that it is 'foreign' rather than local pottery that has usually been discovered in henge ditches suggests that the earthworks were assembly places whose ceremonies were influenced more by new beliefs than by native traditions.

Henges were enclosures and presumably the size of the enclosed space is an indication of the number of people who congregated there. Certainly the largest were built in regions known to be well populated in prehistoric times. The earthworks could be as vast as the Devil's Quoits (II) in Oxfordshire, now ravaged by quarrying but once an enormous oval 165 by 146 metres, an arena into which nearly three thousand participants could have gathered without crowding. Henges could be as little as the unappealingly named Wormy Hillock (I) in Aberdeenshire (Grampian), a mere 17 metres across, whose interior is almost three hundred times tinier than the Devil's Quoits and capable of accommodating no more than seven or eight people comfortably.

Yet, whatever their size, henges were constructed with the simplest of tools: picks and wedges made from antlers, scrapers and rudimentary shovels of ox shoulder-blades, wickerwork baskets and human muscles (figure 8). In an age without metals there was nothing more efficient to use, and the effort demanded to create such earthworks was immense. Today the banks are grass-grown and lowered by weathering. The ditches are two-thirds full of silt and earth and are unimpressive. But excavations at Stonehenge and elsewhere have revealed the careful design of a henge, and how intent the people were to complete the undertaking. There is, however, no evidence that the planners used a national unit of measurement such as Alexander Thom's 'megalithic yard' of 0.83 metre (2 feet 8½ inches). Local yardsticks are more probable.

At Stonehenge men scratched out a furrow for the inner edge of a ditch encircling a space 110 metres across (figure 9). A second furrow marked the ditch's outer rim. A workforce of several gangs of four or five labourers quarried a chain of trenches each about 3 metres long, first slicing off the turf and topsoil for a low outer bank. Then, hammering and wedging the antlers into fissures in the underlying chalk, the diggers prised and hauled out the lumps and fragments for a ditch 1.8 metres deep, scraping the rubble into baskets that were shouldered on to an inner dump, one of many side by side along the rising outline of the high circular bank.

Outer ditches like that at Stonehenge, normal in earthworks of the middle neolithic period, are rare in henges but, interestingly, occur in sites with the earliest dates, at Stonehenge itself, and at Llandegai North in north-west Wales. Most henges had their bank outside the ditch but the result was the same, a great wall so high that no outsider could see into the enclosure.

It has been calculated that four workers, dividing their time between digging and carrying, could extract and shift about 4 tonnes daily. With some 50 tonnes to be removed from each ditch segment, a gang could have completed its section in a fortnight. At Stonehenge there were perhaps a hundred interlocking segments. Fifty working parties could have finished the henge in a month. Two gaps were left for entrances. The depressions between the dumps were filled with earth and broken chalk to smooth the top of the bank but its undulations, like a solidified silhouette of the Loch Ness monster, can still be seen at Stonehenge and other henges.

8. Neolithic tools: an antler 'pick' used for prising out the chalk; an ox shoulder-blade for a scraper or a shovel; and a wickerwork basket. (Photograph: A. Burl.)

9. The low outer and higher inner bank of Stonehenge. The ditch was once 2 metres deep, and the inner bank just as high. (Photograph: A. Burl.)

Although the majority of the earthworks were constructed by this method of linked ditch sections, a system all the more difficult where the trench was to be quarried into bedrock as hard as that at Gorsey Bigbury, there were regional variations. Instead of elongated trenches, deep narrow shafts could be dug like a giant's fingers poked into the ground. At Maumbury Rings in Dorset over forty pits were sunk alongside each other, each an awesome 10 metres deep, with crude steps cut into the sides to enable the workers to clamber out.

In eastern Britain the Type A henges may have had their banks formed from material extracted from outer and inner ditches in order to reduce the need for digging deeply into the ground. The builders of Type C henges in Ireland and the west perhaps chose to scrape up soil from a shallow scooped ramp around the edge of the central space, raising a bank that surrounded a domed area like an upturned dinner-plate, because this was the most economical and quickest way of building a henge. In modern times in Nigeria a workforce of some eighty men very rapidly shifted nearly 500 tonnes of earth to construct a bank 50 metres long and 4 metres high. Arranged in rows of nine or ten, the workers used hoes to scrape the earth backwards between their legs, pushing it from man to man up the rising bank, ending the task in a single day 'by an incredibly intensive effort on the part of the young men'.

Similarly in Ireland, with ox shoulder-blades instead of hoes, people could have scraped up the monstrous ditchless henges. The astonishing Giant's Ring near Belfast, 180 metres across, was surrounded by a bank 20 metres wide and 3.7 metres high, containing some 40,000 tonnes of earth and stone. Employing the Nigerian technique, several score of labourers could have raised even this huge structure in a couple of months.

As well as regional preferences in construction methods there were also differences in size and shape. Double-entranced henges tended to be rather larger than those with one entrance; and whereas the latter were usually circular the former were often irregularly oval. Such non-circular shapes, which appear to be by design rather than by indifference, are intriguing. It has been suggested that the builders wanted to lay out a longer axis, impossible in a circle, to point towards an astronomical event. Alternatively, an oval or egg-shaped enclosure on a hillside could have provided a higher focal point for the ceremonies with spectators standing lower down at the far side of the henge. Some support for this idea comes from the fact that quite often where there are two entrances one is much narrower than the other, one perhaps for the onlookers, the other for those who led the rituals.

The bank was no more than the basic framework of a henge. Inside some of the enclosures, hinting at rites held there, remains have been discovered of settings that for the most part have decayed or been damaged or destroyed. There are remnants of stone circles and timber rings, three-sided structures known as coves, pits, burials, portal stones, features that may have been earlier than, contemporary with or additions made centuries after the construction of the bank. The architecture of henges cannot be contained inside any simple formula.

Nor were henges uniformly spread in Britain and Ireland. Like stone circles, they seem to have been the results of western traditions whose influence weakened increasingly to the east. Even in low-lying areas of easily dug soil their distribution was uneven. In the west of Britain and Ireland they were widely scattered, erected mainly near the coasts where there were patches of fertile lowland. In the most easterly parts of England they were never popular. There, rings of standing posts, carved, coloured, but long since rotted, may have been their timber counterparts.

Elsewhere in England most henges were confined within a narrow north-south band down the centre of the country. The whole of south-east England was a desert for henges. The Midlands and East Anglia had no more than a few. Only the Maiden's Grave at Rudston in Humberside and Arminghall in Norfolk were built near the sea. Otherwise, henges huddled like sheep against the central spine of Britain in a long thin rectangle no more than 32 km (20 miles) wide, from the sheltered eastern hillsides of the Pennines down to the chalk downs of Wessex. Immediately to the west was a comparably condensed band containing the circle-henges where henge and stone-circle zones overlapped.

The activities inside these rings can only be understood by knowing what had happened in prehistoric Britain and Ireland before them.

3
Before henges

Any attempt to explain what henges were demands an explanation of what happened in prehistoric Britain and Ireland before those earthworks were constructed. Henge building began in the centuries before 3000 BC towards the end of the neolithic or new stone age. Before then, for over a thousand years, people had been settling and farming in Britain and Ireland.

By 6000 BC Britain had become an island, separated from the European mainland by the English Channel. The countryside was dark with forests of oaks, elms, birches and pines. Wild animals thrived in them. Into this wilderness the first farmers came around 4500 BC, the remote ancestors of the henge builders.

They were short by today's standards, slightly built, susceptible to accidents and crippling diseases such as arthritis. They were young. Few lived beyond 35 years of age. Yet theirs was a vigorous, enterprising life. Searching for land on the easily worked chalks of southern England, the Yorkshire Wolds, north-eastern Ireland and the rich earths of eastern Scotland, they cut back patches of forest year by year making ever widening territories for themselves.

They had no metals. Their tools were flint, stone, wood, bone, antler, all found within a few miles of the homestead. It was with flint axes that the thick trees were felled to make clearings in which cattle and pigs could graze, and where wheat could be grown on land laboriously tilled by hand. There were no ploughs or traction animals in those early times.

In family holdings of a few square miles of woodland, hillside and stream, the pioneers erected sturdy timbered homes, big enough for them and their livestock. Broken objects recovered by archaeologists suggest that the men farmed, hunted and opened up more land, while the women tended the children, cooked, ground the corn into flour and prepared hides and pelts for skin clothing. There was no weaving, perhaps because there were too few sheep and goats to provide enough wool and hair.

The women made fine hand-shaped, round-bottomed pots along whose rims the impressions of delicate fingertips can be seen. Each region had its own pottery style, and the hollow-shouldered bowls of Yorkshire were different from those of eastern England or Wessex (figure 10).

The burials of these early people have told us much about their way of life and their society. Just as the late neolithic henges in the lowlands and the stone circles on the uplands were architecturally separated by

10. Two early neolithic bowls, coil-built, and round-bottomed to ensure stability on an uneven earthen floor. (Photograph: A. Burl.)

the presence or absence of stone, so the burial places of the first farmers were differentiated by whether it was wood or stone that was plentiful. The earthen long barrows of the east covered timber-built chambers that have long since decayed and collapsed. The megalithic, 'big-stone', long mounds of the west contained massive stone-lined vaults, some of which survive today (figures 11, 12).

A family's barrow apparently was the focus of rites involving a cult of ancestors, as much a temple for the living as a tomb for the dead. The moon was vital. The majority of the long barrows and megalithic tombs had the end under which the bones of the dead lay facing eastwards and the risings of the moon between midsummer and midwinter.

It was a society of equals. But over the centuries death separated some from others. It became customary for only selected people to be buried in what had formerly been communal tombs. Barrows were elaborated to accommodate the bones of the élite. Extra chambers and sidecells replaced the original single vault. Imposing crescentic façades of great stones were erected at the entrance. It seems that burial rites became codified, perhaps led by a chosen member of the group. Fires were lit, funerary feasts were held, offerings were buried in the new and uncovered forecourts of the tombs.

With the expansion of land holdings and an increase in food production came an increase in population. Families linked with families to form clans larger in size and more complex in kinship than the first simple network of individual families. Regional differences blurred. An indication of the growing uniformity amongst societies appeared with the development of an almost national style of pottery known as Peterborough Ware. Its thick-bodied, heavily impressed vessels have been found widely spread over much of England (figure 13).

11. Winterbourne Stoke earthen long barrow, Wiltshire, near Stonehenge. Because Salisbury Plain lacked large stones, such barrows were constructed of chalk and had wooden chambers. (Photograph: A. Burl.)

12. Wayland's Smithy long chambered tomb, Oxfordshire. Where stone was abundant locally, the builders of long barrows used long-lasting sarsen pillars like these. (Photograph: A. Burl.)

13. A Peterborough bowl of the middle neolithic. Such ware, widespread in England, was heavily decorated with impressions. Whipped cord, bird bones, fingernails, even reeds and quills were used. (Photograph: A. Burl.)

Complete self-sufficiency was no longer the ordinary way of life. Single farmsteads gave way to clusters of homes. As fertile unclaimed land became scarcer competition led to rivalry and warfare. Defensive walls, as high as 2 metres at Carn Brea in Cornwall, were erected around emergent villages. Skeletons reveal signs of wounds and of flint arrowheads embedded in bones. Burnt-down entrances to settlements such as Crickley Hill in Gloucestershire tell of attack by fire.

In southern England causewayed enclosures, large hilltop sites surrounded by rings of outer ditches and high protective inner banks, were piled up, the earthworks worn down today by a million rains and frosts. One, perhaps the most famous, enclosing a vast 8 hectares or more, can still be visited at Windmill Hill 1.5 km (1 mile) north-west of Avebury, Wiltshire. Evidence of occupation has been found there and there is also evidence of what is most simply called 'trade'.

Alliances were created as people explored regions beyond their own. Tough stone, ideal for durable axes, was extracted from outcrops and mountainsides in Cornwall, North Wales, the Lake District and Ireland and transported into areas hundreds of miles away. Trackways were established by prospectors and traders. Stretches of navigable rivers eased travel through chaotic forests. Overland paths and waterways interlocked in a tangle of long-distance routes connecting parts of the country that previously had been isolated. It is likely that the causewayed enclosures acted not only as settlements but as staging posts spaced out along these trails, centres where local people and strangers assembled, the times of such seasonal gatherings and ceremonies perhaps determined by the extreme risings or settings of the sun or moon.

This middle neolithic period, from around 3500 BC, with its greater population, its dangers and its valuable products, inevitably saw the rise of leaders who offered safety and security to their followers. So exalted were they that at their deaths only such powerful men received burial in the latest long barrows.

Then there was crisis. Around 3000 BC villages decayed. Wide areas of countryside were deserted. Earthen long barrows and megalithic tombs were abandoned. What had happened is uncertain. Plague is possible; or over-cultivation of the land leading to poor harvests and famine; or a precarious social system wrecked by continual struggle. Whatever it was, the result was a change in the nature of society and its beliefs. For decades there was a Dark Age in prehistoric Britain, a period of confused and fragile evidence before firmer patterns become apparent.

By 2700 BC societies were regrouping, coalescing into bigger, almost sub-tribal units and occupying even larger territories than before. This can be seen most clearly in Wessex, the counties of southern England such as Wiltshire, Dorset and Hampshire. Here, major settlements spaced about 30 km (20 miles) apart have been recognised at Mount Pleasant in Dorset, maybe at Knowlton in the same county, and at

14. A late neolithic Grooved Ware vessel, 18 cm high. This ware was the first flat-based pottery type in Britain. It has often been discovered in henges. (Photograph: A. Burl.)

Durrington Walls near Stonehenge, at Marden and at Avebury in Wiltshire. These huge earthwork enclosures were perhaps the prehistoric
equivalents of political centres. They were not henges.

New cults emerged, one of them associated with pottery known as
Grooved Ware (figure 14), decorated not only with geometrical lines
but sometimes also with potent symbols, spirals, lozenges and rayed
circles, motifs which, as cult images, were adopted eagerly by the leaders.

The personal possessions of these 'chieftains' seem wretchedly poor
today — a perforated antler macehead, a polished axe of attractive
stone, a necklace of wolves' teeth — but they were enough to establish
the man's difference and importance.

Societies were not identical, nor were their beliefs. Homage to ancestors continued strongly in parts of Ireland and the Orkneys. On the
Yorkshire Wolds a form of self-aggrandisement resulted in enormous
and prestigious round barrows being built for the burials of great men.
In Wessex people were attracted by flamboyant ceremonies inside ritual
monuments. But all the areas were linked by the desire for luxury and
display, the acquisition of precious objects and the manipulation of the
forces of nature.

New centres were needed, places where people could gather for fes-
tivals and ceremonies that ensured stability and the continuance of life.
Stone circles were erected in Cumbria and the west. Henges were
constructed in the east and south, not on hilltops like the earlier
causewayed enclosures but on low-lying land near rivers. Circle-henges,
a combination of megalithic ring and circular earthwork, were created
in between the eastern and western zones. All these assembly places
may have been associated with the Grooved Ware cult with its insistence
on the power of ritual deposits.

4
Inside henges

There have been nearly fifty excavations of henges in the twentieth century and the most appropriate verdict for the majority would be: imperfect, incomplete and unsatisfactory. Too often investigators have been content to cut a section through the bank and ditch or open a small square in the interior, leaving nine-tenths of the site untouched.

With such partial excavations it is sometimes difficult to distinguish charms or amulets such as axes or tablets of carved chalk from other articles if they intermingle with the debris of an earlier occupation site. Part of the ditch of the southern earthwork at Llandegai (II), Gwynedd, passed over the postholes of a rectangular building in which there were scatters of early neolithic pottery.

It is also possible to confuse the day-to-day litter of labourers building the henge with objects left inside the completed earthwork. At Dorchester Big Rings, Oxfordshire, 'worshippers lit fires, cooked food and [dropped] broken or chipped pots in both ditches as soon as they had been dug'. The cooking places and squalid shanties of workmen, not worshippers, have been found under the banks of other henges such as Grange in County Limerick. They have no more relevance to the function of the henge than piles of sand and scaffolding on modern building sites.

If the major purpose of a henge was to act as the centre of ceremonial assemblies and rituals of death then its plan and the objects inside it will be different from those of a village. The excavator of the southernmost of the four Priddy henges (IB) (figure 15) in Somerset wrote: 'the most remarkable thing about these excavations is the total absence of any significant deposits or objects.' There was 'not a single grave, burial, sherd of prehistoric or Roman pottery, not a single flint or other stone implement'. The great earthen ring was empty, except for two nodules of marcasite found in a pit on the henge causeway.

These were lustrous bronze-yellow pieces of crystallised iron pyrites from a source no nearer than 40 km (25 miles) or more to the east. Their burial at the entrance may have been an offering of precious articles to enhance the henge. Similar glittering objects have been found with prehistoric burials. The discovery of such strange things at Priddy and elsewhere encourages the belief that henges were for ritual.

So does the orientation of henge entrances. There were regional preferences for direction: north-east in Wessex, cardinal positions in the south-west peninsula, east-west in Ireland. The two adjacent henges (IB, II) at Llandegai, built a thousand years apart, had almost identical alignments to the west-southwest, perhaps looking towards the Febru-

15. The line of three Priddy henges, Somerset, from the north-northeast. All have been damaged by mining. A fourth, unfinished enclosure on the same line is off the photograph to the north. (Photograph: Cambridge University.)

ary sunset of Imbolc, a Celtic festival and today's Candlemas. The width of henge entrances argues against their orientation being for astronomical observation unless there had been a sighting post or stone outside them. Posts have rotted but the massive Heel Stone outside Stonehenge has long been claimed, mistakenly, to be in line with the midsummer sunrise (see chapter 7).

Such sighting devices need not have been for solar or lunar use. Instead, they could have directed the eye towards hills or mountains of special importance to the henge builders. A posthole outside Milfield North (II) in Northumberland marked a low peak in the Cheviots, a similar direction being noticed at the nearby Yeavering (II). 'This might account for the phenomenon of "grouping", different monuments being deliberately sited close together in order to incorporate several different horizon views.'

There are also instances of paired posts or stones like imposing portals on the causeway itself. Entrance posts have been located at Woodhenge (I) and Priddy (IB); stones are recorded as having stood at Mayburgh (IC) and Maumbury Rings (I), and the Slaughter Stone still can be seen, though prostrate, at Stonehenge, the survivor of four towering sarsen pillars that dominated the north-east entrance (figure 16). Henges were intended to impress.

Within many henges aerial photography has revealed the dark marks of rings of grass-grown pits. Two in three of excavated sites are known to have such settings although whether the holes once held upright posts or contained deposits is often uncertain. Without excavation, nothing more is known about the pear-shaped ring at Bow (II) in Devon. Conversely, investigation at Arminghall (IA) in Norfolk uncovered the eight oak postholes of a horseshoe-shaped setting open to the south-

16. An eighteenth-century sketch of the four portal-stones that Inigo Jones had seen in 1620 at Stonehenge's north-east entrance. Only the Slaughter Stone (number 4, left) remains. It has since fallen. (Collection of A. Burl.)

17. Woodhenge, Wiltshire, from the south-west. The flint cairn in the foreground covered the skeleton of a young child whose skull had been split in two. Beyond the cairn the concrete pillars mark the places of former posts. (Photograph: A. Burl.)

west. At North Mains (II) near Crieff in Perthshire (Tayside) 24 large posts had stood in an irregular circle about 25 metres across. At Woodhenge no fewer than six rings were discovered, all elliptical, the posts varying in diameter from 76 cm to 1.5 metres in the third of the rings.

There has been much debate as to whether postholes such as these were the relics of buildings that were once roofed or of free-standing rings of uprights, the timber equivalents of a stone circle. The evidence is equivocal but the writer favours the latter interpretation.

In some henges, however, the pits were dug to receive not posts but offerings. The 56 famous Aubrey Holes at Stonehenge were dug and backfilled, nothing surviving of their contents; reopened, and burnt human bones were buried in them; backfilled and opened yet again to have more cremations put in them together with bone pins, flints and infrequent sherds of Grooved Ware.

At Maumbury Rings near the south coast the 45 incredible shafts had an average depth of 10.4 metres. From each nearly 50 tonnes of chalk was quarried. Carved chalk objects, flints and Grooved Ware lay in the rubble that filled the pits. There were also pig bones from feasts, unused antlers, a worked rib fragment and deer skulls.

The belief that henges were ceremonial enclosures is reinforced by their associated burials, some of which have been considered deliberate sacrifices. A small circle of pits immediately outside the entrance of the north henge at Llandegai (IB) contained a child's cremation. A stone stood on the opposite side of the ring. In the southern henge (II) a central pit 'contained a distinct cremation deposit, perhaps dedicatory itself'. Beyond the western entrance was a cremation pit. A child's corpse buried inside Woodhenge had had its skull cleft in two (figure 17). In the interior of King Arthur's Round Table (II) in Cumbria was a long oblong trench in which a body had been consumed on a fierce hazelwood pyre.

There may even have been an oval mortuary enclosure inside a large henge at Maxey, Cambridgeshire. Built of 156 closely set, squared oak posts, the timber stockade may have safeguarded corpses during periods of mourning. Oddly, it seems to have been burnt down shortly after its erection.

A glimpse of prehistoric pleasure came from one of the 29 burials inside the timber ring of the North Mains henge near Crieff in central Scotland. Analysis of the sediment inside a food-vessel suggested that the pot had contained a fermented drink, perhaps mead or ale or some other alcoholic delight.

Some burials were late additions to a henge. A pit for an urned cremation was dug through a layer of windblown soil that accumulated years after the construction of the Goldington henge (I) in Bedfordshire. But so frequent are the cremations, and in such important positions, by the entrance or at the centre or on the axis, that it is justifiable to regard many as having been part of the rites accompanying the completion of the henge.

The portable objects discovered inside the earthworks also are informative, with native styles of pottery and continental beakers seemingly of marginal importance. Local wares lay in some henges but have been found only rarely on sites along the central spine of Britain, early neolithic sherds coming from a pit not within but outside Coneybury Hill, and a single sherd of Windmill Hill ware from the Stonehenge ditch. Otherwise the pottery has been in outlying henges such as the rusticated ware from Arminghall, Peterborough fragments from Maiden's Grave and Fengate sherds at Castell Bryn-gwyn on Anglesey. In Ireland coarseware has come from Longstone Rath, a Carrowkeel vessel from Monknewton and some coarse flat-bottomed vessels from Grange (IC) in County Limerick.

Where beakers have occurred it has usually been of pots late in the series, and in ditch silts that formed some time after the building of the henge, in secondary layers at sites such as Gorsey Bigbury, Stonehenge

18. An early beaker of the 'European' style, height 14 cm. Such pots originated on the continental mainland. They are believed to have held alcoholic beverages. This pot could have contained over 2 litres. (Photograph: A. Burl.)

and City Farm, where late beaker fragments were found in the upper parts of the ditch.

Strangely, it is only in Ireland, the supposed home of Grooved Ware, that there is any indication that users of beaker pottery may have been responsible for the construction of henges (figure 18). The evidence is inconclusive. At the foot of a high central stone at Longstone Rath a cist contained two cremations and an archer's stone wristguard of a type associated with middle-period beakers. At Micknanstown beaker sherds were found in the southern part of the enclosure; and at Grange several beakers were found with much local Knockadoon ware. There is no direct proof that Beaker people instigated the building of any of these henges.

One type of pottery, however, does appear intimately connected with the archaeology of henges. Grooved Ware has been recovered from several. The vessels are flat-bottomed, poorly fired and decorated in zones of unevenly incised lines in patterns reminiscent of the motifs carved on the kerbs and sideslabs of the passage-tombs of the Boyne valley. An Irish origin, therefore, is feasible, with the added possibility that the vessels are the surviving evidence of an elusive cult that involved complex rites and an esoteric awareness of the moon.

The pots have been found in British henges down the central spine as far north as the Orkneys and as far south as Dorset. Not only were the sherds in the lowest levels of ditches but Grooved Ware seems sometimes to have been placed in special positions. At Wyke Down (I) on Cranborne

Chase, a henge with a ditch formed of interlocking pits like Maumbury Rings 32 km (20 miles) to the south, there were a few sherds in western pits but there was a noticeable concentration of patterned fragments on either side of the entrance at the direct south.

Wyke Down also yielded a collection of chalk objects in the same situation. Such articles, useless as tools, were surely ritual in nature, and their meticulous positioning reveals what is believed to be another aspect of the Grooved Ware cult, the putting together of different things and placing them in selected parts of the henge.

Excavations of some of the deep pits that formed the ditch of Maumbury Rings produced at least seven pieces of carved chalk of whose fertility symbolism there can be little doubt. On the south-east side of the enclosure two shafts contained chalk objects, one a hand-sized chalk block lined with grooves and partly perforated.

Comparable finds have been termed 'cups' or 'lamps' but as the hollows in them are too small for any quantity of liquid much larger than a raindrop, and as there are no signs of burning, the interpretations must be wrong. Because these roughly drilled pieces have been found with chalk carvings of balls and the male penis the associations imply that they represented the female sexual organ (figure 19).

Directly opposite across the henge two other shafts lay on a north-westerly orientation of about 320 degrees towards the moon's most northerly setting. In them were 'carved chalk objects', of which one was an unmistakable phallus. Also found at Maumbury Rings were a

19. Small chalk ritual objects. There are two male phalli in the foreground. Rear left is a chalk 'cup'. On the right is an incised plaque. Associations suggest these fetishes were fertility symbols. (Photograph: A. Burl.)

chalk ball, now lost, and some little chalk plaques with tidily patterned lines like the designs on Grooved Ware.

What is remarkable about these pieces is not only their Grooved Ware and lunar associations. Their potency may have been enhanced by the antlers that were buried with them. The phenomenon of deer shedding antlers and regrowing them may, to the prehistoric mind, have made the antler a powerful symbol of rebirth. Unused antlers were purposely laid at the bottom of several henge ditches.

Fertility and astronomy may have merged at a newly discovered henge at Shepperton (I) in Surrey. The north-east entrance, guarded by a human skeleton, faced the midsummer sunrise. In the ditch a deposit of red ochre was buried in line with the southern moonrise, and between it and the moon's most southerly setting an arc of red-deer antlers had been carefully laid along the ditch bottom.

In regions beyond the chalklands of Wessex similar pieces are almost non-existent. If made of wood they have disintegrated although one tiny hermaphroditic figurine of ashwood with breasts and penis was preserved in the Somerset fens.

A few flints have come from henges such as Castilly (I). Burnt flints lay in the postholes at Arminghall. In each of the Llandegai henges was a pit with small stones, one 'a handful of conspicuously marked pebbles'. Although such non-utilitarian deposits in henges were clearly deliberate their meaning is probably beyond recovery.

Fertility symbolism in henges, however, was not confined to Wessex and to chalk. The contents of two small enclosures, now destroyed, at Maxey near Stamford proved this. Grooved Ware sherds were recovered from the excavations. In the ditch of the smaller henge archaeologists unearthed an antler coloured with red ochre and incised with criss-cross chevron motifs that duplicated the geometrical patterns on many Grooved Ware vessels.

From the outer ditch of the western henge (IA) came a similarly grooved antler. In the inner ditch was an elaborately treated deer rib, smoothed, its upper part decorated with grooved chevrons in which red ochre could still be seen. Black colouring of soot or crushed charcoal covered the outer side, the black joining the red in a straight line. 'The association of the three objects within sacred monuments suggests....that they served a ritual purpose.' None of this could be domestic refuse thrown away inside a henge.

Despite the decay of timber settings inside many of these henges, the posts perhaps brightly painted and enriched with arcane carvings, it is clear that ritual was central to these overgrown earthworks.

The monstrous settings of standing stones inside some of them confirm that these were places for special occasions.

5
The circle-henges

Immediately west of the line of henges that extends north-south down the central spine of Britain is a band of henges containing stone circles. They occupy a narrow zone where eastern henge and western stone-circle traditions overlapped. The most northerly of these circle-henges is the Ring of Brodgar (II) on Orkney. A thousand kilometres (620 miles) to the south on Bodmin Moor are the Stripple Stones (I).

Most of these hybrid monuments are in Britain, with others such as Castleruddery (IC) and Grange (IC) in Ireland. There may have been a further Scottish site at the tiny Contin henge (I) in Ross and Cromarty (Highland) but if so the stones of its circle were removed before 1822.

Perhaps because of the attraction of their megalithic rings, most have been extensively excavated. Brodgar is an exception. Standing near trackways or by rivers, the majority are large, their interiors rarely less than 46 metres across.

Several facts attest to their funerary associations. Some have central burials. Others such as Arbor Low, Derbyshire, and Stonehenge lie at the heart of a dispersed ring of chambered tombs and round barrows. Three, Arbor Low (II), Cairnpapple (II) in West Lothian and Stenness (I) in Orkney, had three-sided settings of standing stones inside them (figure 20). Known as *coves*, these unroofed structures have been interpreted as imitations of early neolithic burial chambers, and it is possible that mourners gathered there, their rites no longer performed inside the dark claustrophobia of a tomb but in the open air of a henge. It is even possible that the circle-henges were erected around an existing cove. Free-standing examples of these 'chambers' exist well outside the stone circles of Avebury and Stanton Drew in Wessex, and to the west of the Meini-gwyr (IC) circle-henge in south-west Wales.

The stone circles inside these henges are rarely plain. A centre stone stood inside the Stripple Stones. Other rings had portals flanking the henge entrances. Avenues of earth or stone led to Stonehenge and Broomend of Crichie, perhaps even to Arbor Low and Stenness.

Circle-henges may have been monuments of several distinct phases. Grooved Ware lies in the ditches of some henges but never in the stoneholes of the internal circles which may have been put up years after the construction of the earthwork. This was true at Stonehenge, where two concentric rings of doleritic Welsh bluestone were erected at least a thousand years after the henge. At other sites the plan of the rings seldom conforms to the line of the ditch, as though the two features were laid out at separate times. At Cairnpapple and Arbor Low,

20. The cove inside Stenness circle-henge, Orkney. The fallen slab once stood a metre behind its separated partners in an open-air version of the walls of a chamber inside nearby megalithic tombs. (Photograph: A. Burl.)

21. The impressive stones of the Ring of Brodgar circle-henge, Orkney. The rim of the encircling ditch can just be seen in the foreground. (Photograph: A. Burl.)

two sites which are noticeably similar despite being 300 km (186 miles) apart, the henges are oval but the stone 'circles' are egg-shaped, each with an axis different from that of the surrounding bank. At the Devil's Quoits the outline of the ditch, distorted like a badly dented frying-pan, enclosed an almost perfect circle of standing stones.

Today few of the rings are in good condition. Those at Stonehenge were uprooted and, centuries later, rearranged in horseshoe-shaped settings. The circles at the Devil's Quoits, Balfarg and the Bull Ring (II) near Buxton were destroyed. Stenness and Stripple Stones were pillaged for building material. Of the six stones once inside Broomend of Crichie four were robbed. To compound confusion, a nearby pillar with Dark Age Pictish carvings was added to the henge to avoid destruction by nineteenth-century railway workers.

To have any idea of how magnificent these circle-henges once were, it is necessary to go to Grange in County Limerick or to the Ring of Brodgar on Orkney (figure 21), where 27 elegant pillars of sandstone survive of an original sixty, the tallest a full 5.6 metres high.

Otherwise the rings have been devastated. So tumbled and untidy are the stones inside Arbor Low that there are doubts that they ever stood upright (figure 22). Careful inspection, however, shows that one at the

22. Arbor Low circle-henge, Derbyshire. In the centre is a collapsed cove. The circle-stones are fallen but once were erect. (Photograph: A. Burl.)

west-southwest still leans and that ankle-high stumps of others are still erect. Like its Scottish counterpart at Cairnpapple, Arbor Low never had more than the shallowest of sockets for its stones. Rains, frosts and gusting winds across the exposed bleakness of the Peak District have thrown the circle down.

There is an intriguing but probably mistaken coincidence about the numbers of stones in these rings. From Brodgar, where there may once have been sixty stones, down to the Stripple Stones with a possible thirty, the builders may have counted in multiples of six. Broomend of Crichie did have six stones. Stenness had twelve. The inner and outer rings at Balfarg have been computed at twenty-four and twelve respectively. Twenty-four has been suggested for Cairnpapple, thirty-six for Arbor Low, and the same number for the Devil's Quoits.

Before any mathematical deductions are made it must be stressed that these are nearly all estimates. Stoneholes have been lost by quarrying. Others have never been excavated. And Stonehenge, ever the megalithic maverick, is supposed to have had thirty-eight stones in each of its two circles, a number of no interest whatsoever to a believer in a prehistoric counting-base of six.

One point of astronomical interest is that at the Stones of Stenness, excavated in 1973-4, there had been a neat circle of stones (figure 23). It stood inside a henge with a single entrance at the north by which Grooved Ware sherds were found in the ditch. Of the expected twelve stones there was 'no good evidence' that one had ever been put up, and a gap may have been intentionally left there in the ring. The space was at the south-east, where the midwinter sun rose over the hills 5 km (3 miles) away.

That the history of these circle-henges may have been long and involved is shown by Balfarg near Markinch in Fife, a site now preserved and partly reconstructed. It was excavated in 1977-8.

A perfectly circular ditch and bank enclosed an area about 60 metres across. A cardinal entrance may have existed at the south. There was certainly a narrow entrance at the west-northwest, beyond which the minor moon would have set over the Lomond Hills 5 km (3 miles) away. This, however, was a celestial position so difficult to make out amongst all the other lunar settings in the northern sky that it must be questionable whether prehistoric people were able to identify it — or even be aware of its existence.

The moon has a regular 18.61 year cycle during which, like a lunar pendulum, it steadily swings from a major to a minor position and back again at all four of its northern (midwinter) and southern (midsummer) risings and settings. At Balfarg its major setting was at the north-west. Then, over the next nine years, it moved ever further down the skyline

23. The surviving stones of Stenness, Orkney. The local sandstone splits naturally into elegantly rectangular pillars. In the middle background are the low slabs of the cove. (Photograph: A. Burl.)

until at its minor setting at the west-northwest it would have been hard to distinguish amongst the other monthly settings between north-west and south-west.

Inside the henge and near the west-northwest entrance what appears to have been a dedicatory ceremony took place before the erection of a circle of heavy posts. Four radiocarbon determinations averaging 2250 bc (*c*.2900 BC) date this episode firmly. Fires were lit, wood and bones were burned and Grooved Ware vessels smashed in a restricted area just to the west of where the ring of posts would stand. Then sixteen timbers were erected in a circle 25 metres across, the posts rising in height towards the entrance. Inside the ring there may have been as many as five more circles of much slighter posts. These have been tentatively interpreted as supports for flimsy hurdlework fencing to conceal the central rites from anyone outside.

Over the years the posts weathered. They were replaced by two stone circles, an outer of twenty-four stones, an inner of twelve, with two heavy portals at the entrance. The concentric rings may have been longer-lasting replicas in stone of the timber rings. Such megalithic reproduction of wooden prototypes is known in other stone circles.

The stones, significantly, did not repeat the alignment of the henge. Instead, like the recumbent stone circles of Aberdeenshire (Grampian) to the north, they were graded in height towards the south-west, another indication that henge builders and stone-circle builders did not share identical beliefs.

There was the faintest of hints that in their shapes the stones had been selected to alternate between thin pillar and plump lozenge like those of the Kennet Avenue at Avebury which have been thought to represent male and female principles. Such fertility symbolism would not be out of place in modern thinking about henges.

At some time the corpse of an adolescent, probably male, was buried in a pit near the middle of the circle and covered with an enormous 1.5 tonne capstone (figure 24). Near his hand stood a gross, handled beaker, like an oversized beer mug, with a capacity of 1.7 litres (3 pints). Whether his death was by sacrifice, accident or natural causes, he had been given adequate and comfortable sustenance for the afterlife.

Burials, the moon, stone circles — all these strengthen the interpretation of circle-henges as monuments for ritual rather than for occupation or defence. In this they differed from the great earthwork enclosures such as Avebury and Mount Pleasant in Wessex.

24. A nineteenth-century sketch of a beaker burial in Wiltshire. A similar skeleton with its liquid-filled beaker was found at Balfarg circle-henge, Fife. (Collection of A. Burl.)

6
The great earthwork enclosures

Enclosing a space by erecting an earthen bank around it was a common-place building technique in neolithic times. It no more distinguished a henge from a settlement site than the use of bricks and mortar distin-guishes a modern town hall from a cinema or even a public house.

What separates a henge from monuments of similar construction is not its architecture but its associations. Except perhaps for their size henges are indistinguishable in appearance from the bewildering range of late neolithic and early bronze age earthworks, domestic or defensive, diminutive or sprawling, that are scattered across the lowlands of Brit-ain. In Ireland they are architecturally camouflaged amongst the thou-sands of raths, near-circular forts of one or more earthen banks and ditches, erected from the late bronze age to as late as the thirteenth century AD.

In Britain and Ireland there are banked enclosures far too small ever to have held a congregation. There are others so large that they could have accommodated forty thousand people, probably a greater part of the population of England at that time.

If accepted as places of assembly, henges can be allotted an arbitrary range in diameter from as little as 15 metres to as large as 150 metres. Earthworks beyond those limits may be presumed to have had alterna-tive functions. Wormy Hillock (see chapter 2) at the lower end of the scale could have held seven or eight people but some sites are very much smaller. Tiny earthworks like Ring E at Llandegai can be excluded. So can the double-entranced Fargo Plantation just north of Stonehenge. Its central space was less than 4.6 metres across, too cramped for a couple to dance even a slow waltz in comfort. At its centre was a rectangular grave with a skull-less skeleton, cremations, food-vessels and a late beaker. It was a burial place. Despite the bank, ditch and entrance, its excavator, J. F. S. Stone, in his *Wessex before the Celts* (1958), rejected it as a henge. It and others like it 'may simply be anomalous graves built on the lines of the larger and more formal "temples"'.

Equally to be denied the status of henges are the great earthwork enclosures of Wessex. These are so expansive and contain so much evidence of permanent occupation that they are better interpreted as settlement sites. Some of them even have a henge or its equivalent inside the embankment. Others have henges alongside them.

There are five of these giant enclosures in southern England: Mount Pleasant and Knowlton in Dorset, and Durrington Walls, Marden and

Avebury in Wiltshire. To these can be added comparable enclosures at Waulud's Bank in Bedfordshire, Meldon Bridge near Peebles (Borders) and Forteviot in Perthshire (Tayside). More remain to be recognised.

They are enormous. Whereas a large henge might have an interior of 0.6 ha the average of these vast compounds is fifteen times greater. The smallest, at Mount Pleasant, encompasses 4.6 ha, and the misshapen horseshoe at Marden abutting the river Avon, enclosed 14 ha, as capacious as a car park for sixteen thousand vehicles.

Several, like Marden, were near rivers, Durrington Walls by the Avon, Avebury close to the Kennet, and Waulud's Bank adjoining the Lea. At that site hundreds of flint arrowheads were found, suggestive of large-scale hunting or, more probably, warfare.

Excavations have shown that several of the enclosures were put up on land where there had been a previously undefended settlement, and it may have been the changing, uneasy times of the late neolithic that led to the savagely deep ditches of the new earthworks. Durrington Walls had a ditch 12 metres wide and 6 metres deep, and at Avebury ditches no less than 9 metres deep were quarried down into the solid chalk (figure 25). Outside these ditches were monstrous banks up to 6 metres

25. The weathered bank and ditch of the Avebury earthwork enclosure, Wiltshire. The ditch was once almost sheer-sided and nearly 10 metres deep. (Photograph: A. Burl.)

high. At Meldon Bridge 3.4 ha of forest were felled for the timbers of a massive defensive wall 500 metres long that cut off a promontory between a river and its tributary. Mount Pleasant had a towering oak palisade around it. These were laboriously constructed defences, but it has been claimed that the banks could not have been for protection because, unlike hillforts, they had internal ditches. Yet if cattle and other livestock were kept inside the enclosures the deterrent of an inner ditch would have safeguarded them more surely than an inner bank from whose top they could have slipped and tumbled down the steep sides on to the bottom of a precipitously deep outlying ditch.

Excavations by St George Gray at Avebury (1908-22), by Dyer at Waulud's Bank (1953, 1971), and by Burgess at Meldon Bridge (1974-5) have produced evidence of domestic use, of pottery, especially Grooved Ware, worked flints, tools, hearths, rubbish pits and houses. The postholes of impressive timber structures were discovered during the equally impressive excavations by Geoffrey Wainwright, whose book, misleadingly entitled *The Henge Monuments* (1989), clearly and excitingly describes his investigations at Durrington Walls (1966-8), Marden (1969) and Mount Pleasant (1970-1). There was Grooved Ware in all of them, and there were the remains of large circular structures. At Durrington Walls geophysical surveys detected the former existence of at least seventeen other rings, probably the traces of houses in a village like an African kraal.

In Wessex these colossal earthworks seem to have acted as territorial centres, and they may have been the successors of the nearby earlier, smaller causewayed enclosures, also domestic and defensive in nature. Maiden Castle causewayed camp was near Mount Pleasant, Hambledon Hill near Knowlton South, Robin Hood's Ball not far from Durrington Walls, and the half-abandoned site of Windmill Hill overlooked Avebury. The causewayed enclosure of Maiden Bower was only 6 km (4 miles) from Waulud's Bank.

Just as today's cities have cemeteries and churches inside them so these great earthwork enclosures had great round barrows and henges in or near them, another reason for denying them any role as henges.

The Conquer Barrow, 2.7 metres high and 30 metres across, was erected on the bank of Mount Pleasant. Knowlton South lay just 180 metres from the Great Barrow, still 6 metres high and 38 metres in diameter. The huge Hatfield Barrow, 'the Giant of Marden', collapsed inside the earthwork in an avalanche of sand during the eighth day of excavation in 1807. 1.5 km (1 mile) south of Avebury the almost unbelievably man-made, chalk Silbury Hill (figure 26) rises an incredible 40 metres high, its base alone covering 2.2 ha, almost four times the area of a big henge. The significance of these man-made mounds, like

26. Silbury Hill, Wiltshire. This man-made mound, 40 metres high, is only 1.2 km (³/₄ mile) south of Avebury. (Photograph: A. Burl.)

burial places of the gods, remains unclear. Their proximity to the enclosures, however, is an indication that the function of the earthworks themselves was the mundane one of occupation and defence.

This is reinforced by the fact that henges and rings were sometimes built inside the enclosures. One of the large structures inside Durrington Walls has been interpreted as a ceremonial council house although architectural analysis favours the idea of a free-standing ring of posts. At Durrington Walls, moreover, there is a henge, Woodhenge, immediately outside the south entrance and there are two others within 3 km (2 miles) at Coneybury Hill and Stonehenge.

Ritual settings were found inside Meldon Bridge. Forteviot, near Perth, had two henges, one inside the post-lined enclosure, another just outside the north-northwest entrance. A henge inside Mount Pleasant enclosed several rings of postholes. Knowlton South, 244 metres across, lay close to the henge (II), inside which a medieval church was to be built (figure 27). Preceding the awesome ditch and bank at Avebury were two gigantic stone circles, around which the earthwork was constructed years later.

Cumulatively the evidence is insistent that the great earthwork enclosures were settlement sites, put up against navigable rivers but with daunting banks and ditches for protection. Despite the fire that destroyed the stockade at Mount Pleasant shortly after it was erected, people could expect to live safely in these huge sites.

The enclosures might contain henges or stone circles, the ritual assembly places of the people, or they might have these assembly places alongside them. They were not henges themselves.

27. The Knowlton complex, Dorset. In the foreground is part of the earthwork enclosure, the dark line of its ditch enclosing farm buildings. To its north is the henge with a church inside it. The tree-covered Great Barrow is to its east. Round barrows can be made out around the henge. (Photograph: J. Boyden.)

7
Stonehenge and Woodhenge

These famous sites reveal how tantalising an uninformed visit to a henge can be and how deceptive a henge's bland emptiness is. Both had astronomical alignments built into them and both had objects buried in carefully chosen locations. These articles are now in the museums of Salisbury and Devizes.

Stonehenge is almost a thousand years older than Woodhenge, its inner and outer banks being constructed around 3200 BC by natives of Salisbury Plain, the descendants of the long-barrow builders. A narrow causeway lay at the exact south, with a second, wider entrance at the north-east. Beyond it rose the gross bulk of the Heel Stone (figure 28).

This outlier is popularly thought to stand in line with the midsummer sunrise but it does not and never did. To be in the correct place it should be a full 1.8 metres to the north. Astronomical analysis has shown that, instead, the stone is in line with the rising of the moon halfway between its northern minor and major positions. It is unlikely to be coincidental that the western edge of the henge entrance was in line with the major rising while its eastern side marked the midpoint of the lunar cycle (figure 29).

The chances of the alignment being fortuitous were virtually extinguished by the discovery in 1922 of six straggling rows of postholes across the entrance itself. They were too close-set to have supported gates but it was more than forty years before 'Peter' Newham's brilliant perception explained their purpose. They had been sighting posts set up to mark the shifting risings of the moon year by year, a process continued until observers were certain of how far to the north the moon rose. In this they continued the centuries-old practices of long-barrow builders who had laid out their burial mounds towards the moon as a part of their funerary beliefs.

With the Heel Stone marking the midpoint of the lunar cycle, the Stonehenge people knew that when the moon reappeared to the left of the pillar it would reach its northern extreme four years later. Great posts were erected as astronomical signposts in the gap between the stone and the major moonrise.

The sun, apparently, did not interest the henge builders. It may have been the users of beakers who converted Stonehenge into a solar monument. Struggles between vying cults are not unknown in prehistory. A thousand years after the building of the earthwork people widened the north-east entrance by throwing a long section of the bank back into the ditch (figure 30). The effect was to have the Heel Stone stand almost at the centre of the causeway as though indicating the place of midsummer sunrise. The line of posts had gone and there was little to show that the henge had been a place of the moon.

Perhaps two hundred years before this there had been another change. People, maybe newcomers, dug the 56 pits called the Aubrey Holes around the inside of the bank. They also emphasised the importance of various positions in the henge by the burial of chosen deposits. The base of a Grooved Ware pot was placed in an Aubrey Hole at the south-west end of the lunar axis; a beautiful stone macehead (figure 31) was set in line with the major southern moonrise; at the north-eastern entrance antlers were put in an Aubrey Hole and the corpses of an adult and child were buried in the ditch alongside the causeway. In the ditch on one side of the south entrance were Grooved Ware sherds.

On the other side was a second burial of an adult and child. A chalk ball and some viciously sharp flint knives were concealed in the neighbouring Aubrey Holes. The cult reserved such offerings exclusively for the entrances and the lunar orientations. None was found elsewhere.

As well as the ball of chalk, a chalk axe was discovered in the henge but it was in a disturbed stonehole and nothing can be deduced about its original position. Two other chalk axes, however, were found at Woodhenge 3 km (2 miles) away and here the evidence for astronomy and meticulous deposition is stronger still.

28. The Heel Stone at Stonehenge. It may have been set up to indicate the course of the rising moon in the northern sky. (Photograph: A. Burl.)

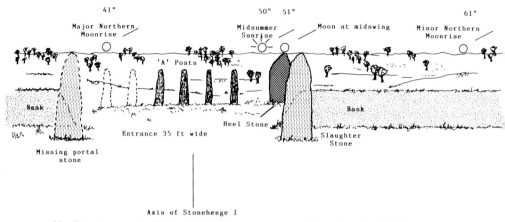

29. Stonehenge: the first, narrow north-east entrance. (Drawing: A. Burl.)

Woodhenge was the first site to be discovered from the air. It was excavated by the Cunningtons in 1926-7. The earthwork consisted of an irregular bank and ditch. Inside were six concentric ovals of postholes. Their axis did not respect the henge's north-northeast entrance. Instead it pointed north-eastwards towards the midsummer sunrise. Two slender sighting posts had been set up when planning the new alignment. It is possible, therefore, that the timber ovals and the earthwork were of different periods. Two carbon-14 assays from material in the ditch bottom, where Grooved Ware lay, gave 'dates' of 1805±54 bc and 1867±74 bc, around 2280 BC. The rings may be later, associated with beaker sherds in the upper levels of the ditch.

30. Stonehenge: the widened north-east entrance. (Drawing: A. Burl.)

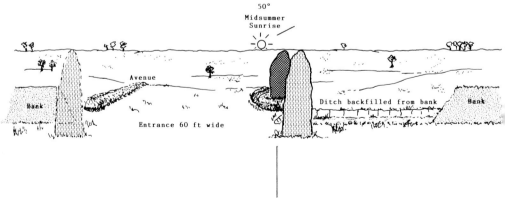

31. The lovely macehead from Stonehenge. Made of Scottish hornblendic gneiss, it is 5.25 cm long. It was found with the cremated bones of a child. (Photograph: A. Burl.)

The builders seem to have used a unit of measurement, the 'beaker yard' of 73 cm (2 feet 4³/₄ inches) when laying out the rings. Maud Cunnington, the excavator, thought they had used a 'short foot' of 29 cm (11¹/₂ inches), and Alexander Thom suggested that his 'megalithic yard' of 0.83 metre (2 feet 8¹/₂ inches) had been the unit. Neither of these fits as well as the 'beaker yard'.

Table 2. The long diameters of the six rings at Woodhenge.

Ring	F	E	D	C	B	A
Imperial feet	38.4	57.6	76.8	96.0	125.0	144.0
Metres	11.7	17.6	23.4	29.3	38.1	43.9

Theoretical prehistoric measures

	F	E	D	C	B	A
Cunnington, 'short foot': 29 cm (11¹/₂ inches)	40.1	60.1	80.1	100.2	130.5	150.3
Thom, 'megalithic yard': 0.83 metre (2 feet 8¹/₂ inches)	14.1	21.2	28.2	35.3	46.0	52.9
Burl, 'beaker yard': 73 cm (2 feet 4³/₄ inches)	16.0	24.0	32.0	40.0	52.1	60.0

According to Cunnington the rings were spaced 2.9 metres (9 feet 7 inches) apart. That this should be the precise equivalent of 4 'beaker yards' is mathematically very suggestive, with so many other multiples of four in the measurements.

It is likely that other timber rings were planned using units of measurement that varied locally. At North Mains the circle's assumed diameter of 25 metres (82 feet) corresponds closely to 30 of Thom's megalithic yards. Possibly by chance, only 35 km (22 miles) to the east the timber ring inside Balfarg was of the same dimensions. But it is only when there are several concentric rings, as at Woodhenge, all of which fit a

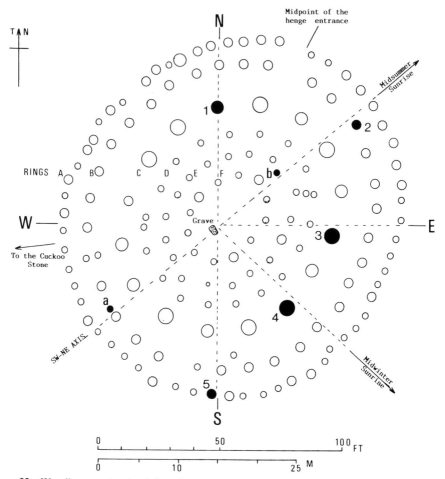

32. Woodhenge: the ritual deposits: 1, the only cremation; 2, chalk axe and worked chalk; 3, chalk 'cup' and worked chalk; 4, chalk 'cup' and worked chalk; 5, chalk axe and worked chalk; a, b, sighting posts for the midsummer sunrise. (Drawing: A. Burl.)

proposed unit, that any deduction can safely be made.

There has been much argument as to whether the posts at Woodhenge supported a roof and, despite architectural opinion, it has generally been accepted that the rings had been covered, perhaps with an open space at the centre. There are reasons for disbelieving this. The rings are not quite oval but egg-shaped with the broader end at the south-west. There is no structural explanation for this but there is a social one. It may have been at the wider south-west that spectators gathered to watch ceremonies performed at the far end of the axis, looking towards the rising midsummer sun. If so, a walled and roofed building would have hidden the phenomenon from them. Free-standing rings of posts are more feasible and, arguably, not all of the same period.

Roofed or unroofed, Woodhenge is vital to the question of a henge's purpose because of the ritual objects found in it and because of the manner in which they were used to mark both cardinal and calendrical points (figure 32).

North, east, south and west all had special deposits buried in postholes on their alignments, possibly before the posts were erected. The only cremation in the whole site lay in the northernmost hole of Ring C, an oval of the heaviest posts and the third from the outside. East was recorded by a chalk 'cup' and a piece of worked chalk in a hole of the same ring. A skeleton of a young man was buried in the ditch on the same line. An axe of chalk and a crude disc of perforated chalk lay at the south in a posthole of the outer ring, A. Just west of the centre of Woodhenge there was a slight post, and 400 metres beyond it was the Cuckoo Stone, now prostrate, but once a tall sarsen standing in line with the equinoctial sunset.

The disposition of these deposits was selective. Maud Cunnington dug to the bottom of every one of the 156 postholes at Woodhenge but it was only in the five cardinal or calendrical pits that unique objects such as chalk axes or 'cups' were found. That they had been deliberately concealed is also unquestionable. Cunnington herself remarked that 'these chalk objects if exposed to a hard frost would go to pieces in a single night, and they must therefore have been buried intentionally... very soon after they were made.'

Two chalk axes were recorded from Woodhenge. It has been supposed that the axe, whether of usable stone or fragile chalk, was the symbol of a guardian of the dead just as the Christian cross is the symbol of the Crucifixion. For this reason it is interesting to note where the two were found. One was in the southern posthole of Ring A. The other was in a hole of the second ring, B. It lay on the alignment to the midsummer sunrise.

A chalk 'cup' in Ring C was on the orientation of the midwinter sunrise. It is the repetition of deposits in such significant places and their total exclusion elsewhere, and never in the innermost three rings, that confirms the interpretation of Woodhenge as a ritual enclosure.

Each of the postholes where these articles lay was just off the alignment as though to permit viewers to look along the sightline. It is another reason for rejecting the idea of an enclosed building.

Woodhenge may even have been sanctified by sacrifice. Near the centre of the rings, lying across the axis, the visitor will see a small oval heap of flints. It covered a grave. The pit contained the skeleton of a very young child facing the midsummer sunrise. Its skull had been split in two.

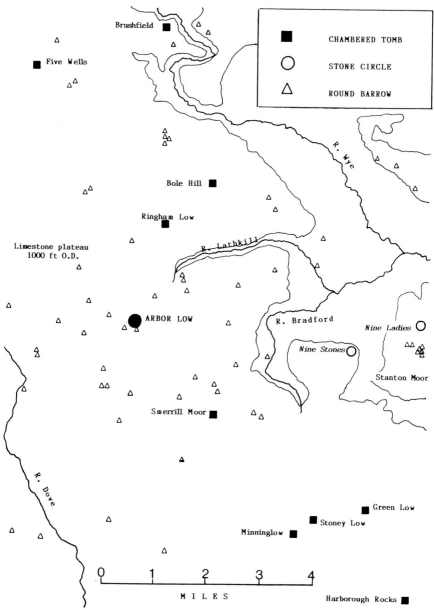

33. Arbor Low: the long and round barrows around the circle-henge. (Drawing: A. Burl.)

8
Function

Henges were a lowland phenomenon, and one that was largely re-stricted to Britain. There may be only a few henges in Ireland, and almost none on islands. There are just two henges in the Orkneys and not one in the Scillies or in Shetland. The remote ends of Britain were unaffected by the concept of enclosed assembly places. There the traditional cults of ancestors and megalithic tombs continued uninter-rupted.

It was on the mainlands that henges were erected as novel but essen-tial ritual centres. Some indication of their importance comes from the special treatment given to the gravel banks of the three Thornborough henges. All were deliberately coated with crystals of gypsum, rendering them vividly white against the countryside.

It is becoming clear that these simple enclosures were anything but simple and were places of elaborate, perhaps awesome complexity to their people. Excavations can recover very little of the evanescent ceremonies performed there. Only the alignments, the carved chalk, the broken potsherds survive of the rites. Everything else is lost or forgotten.

Henges were the focal points of what had been a scatter of family and clan territories in the prehistoric landscape. They superseded the role of the old neolithic long barrows and became the focus of the round bar-rows of the early bronze age. Many were built in the middle of an area cluttered with abandoned burial places. Stonehenge had sixteen earthen long barrows within 5 km (3 miles) of it. Arbor Low was constructed at the heart of a ring of deserted megalithic tombs (figure 33). And both, like the majority of their counterparts, had round barrows clustering around them as though the henge had been the stage for funerary rites. There were at least 28 bronze age barrows around the Thornborough earthworks.

With Irish henges the connection with death and the past is even more explicit. The earthworks around the Boyne Valley were put up alongside passage-tombs. The Giant's Ring in County Down had a megalithic tomb inside it. By Lough Erne in County Fermanagh a stone-banked, ditchless ring enclosed the Moylehid passage-tomb.

At Longstone Rath near Naas in County Kildare a blazing brushwood fire, like a beacon, was lit on a hill summit conspicuous for miles around. 'No trace of human or animal remains, bone or shell, nor any scrap of pottery was found in this burnt stratum. This clearly proved we had not to deal with camp- or cooking-fires.... One can only assume

34. The surviving stone of a four-poster stone circle inside Mayburgh circle-henge, Cumbria. The henge bank is composed of hundreds of thousands of water-worn cobbles. (Photograph: A. Burl.)

that here was an important religious centre.' When the flames died down the bodies of a man and a woman were cremated in a long cist at the foot of a towering granite pillar. Around it, in an exact circle, the bank and outer ditch of the henge were laid out. Like the 'burials' at Balfarg and Llandegai and elsewhere, the cremations may have been dedications, even sacrifices, made at the inauguration of the henge.

It is likely that henges were connected with the 'trade' in stone axes. Some, like Mayburgh, King Arthur's Round Table and Meini-gwyr, were near 'factory' sources. Castlewitch in Cornwall was close to an outcrop on Balston Down. The Thornborough henges occupied an area from which Cumbrian axes were redistributed into the Peak District and Wessex. At Cairnpapple near Edinburgh flakes of foreign axes from Cumbria and North Wales were discovered inside the earthwork. At Llandegai, close to the Graig Lwyd 'factory', a fragment of stone from south-west Wales showed signs of polishing, and at the same site a Cumbrian axe in mint condition had been buried blade-down in the henge. 'The unused axe and well-used polisher brought from distant parts of western Britain can only have ritual meaning when considered against the very nearness of one of the most prolific sources of axe material at Graig Lwyd.'

In the late nineteenth century a stone axe was found buried at the entrance to Mayburgh (figure 34). The cult may even have endured into the early bronze age. There is an eighteenth-century record of a 'brass celt' — a bronze axe — being dug up in the same area. The conclusion that natives and strangers gathered in henges at particular times of the year for transactions concerned with the axe in its dual role as tool and life/death symbol would explain the mixture of the mundane and the sacred suspected for many of the activities within the enclosures.

The axe, the sun and moon, funerary rites, timber rings and stone circles, articles buried in chosen places, enclosed spaces for seasonal ceremonies, all are aspects of henges in a tradition that endured for over a thousand years. But by 2000 BC it was over. New beliefs developed. Henges were abandoned.

Some like Castell Bryn-gwyn were transformed into forts. Castilly became an open-air theatre for medieval plays. Knowlton had a church built inside it (figure 35). The Giant's Ring was used as a racecourse. Thornhaugh in Northamptonshire was turned into a water garden.

35. The Christianisation of a pagan henge. This aerial view of Knowlton, Dorset, shows the ruins of a twelfth-century church inside it. (Photograph: J. Boyden.)

Maumbury Rings underwent constant change: a Roman amphitheatre, a 1643 Civil War gun battery, the site of an eighteenth-century gallows. In 1705 ten thousand spectators watched as Mary Channing was partly suffocated and then burned for poisoning her husband. As if these transmutations were not enough, the henge would have been demolished in 1857 to make way for a railway had it not been for the public outcry led by William Barnes, the poet.

Some henges were venerated. Another name for the village of Bow in Devon with its great henge is Nymet Tracey, Tracey being the surname of the landowner, William, one of the four knights who murdered Thomas à Becket in 1170. Nymet is a corruption of the Latin *nemeton* or 'sacred place'. Near Bow are several other *nemeton* placenames, suggesting that the henge was regarded as holy even in historical times.

Other henges were venerated but then vandalised. In the late seventeenth century the Muir of Ord, the small double-entranced earthwork between the Beauly and Conon rivers, was so respected that 'all who live near it hold it as sacred, and will not cut so much as a rod out of it'. It was still untouched in 1883. Today its interior has been levelled for one of the greens on a golf course. A low mound at its centre, perhaps covering a burial, has been flattened. A gap has been cut through the bank 'for the convenience of golfers'.

As the players engage in the ritual of depositing a chalky white ball into a hole carefully positioned inside the henge one wonders if they sense faint mocking laughter somewhere on the green.

9
Glossary

Barrow: an artificial mound of earth, chalk or turf used to cover one or more burials.

Beakers: distinctive and elaborately decorated flat-bottomed pots, originally of continental origin. The vessels were often burnished. The style appeared in Britain in the late neolithic period. It is conventional to divide the tradition into three phases: **early**, beginning around 2500 BC; **middle**, 2400 to 2100 BC; and **late**, ending around 1900 BC.

Boyne Valley: an area by the river Boyne in eastern Ireland in which an important passage-tomb cemetery was built.

Cairn: like a barrow but composed of stones.

Carrowkeel ware: a native form of Irish neolithic pottery, often found in passage-tombs.

Causewayed enclosure: once known as causewayed camps, these middle neolithic hilltop settlements were surrounded by irregular rings of one or more banks and ditches.

Circle-henge: a henge with a stone circle inside it.

Cist: a grave lined with thin slabs and covered by a capstone.

Cove: a late neolithic three-sided setting of upright stones, usually open to the east. They have been likened to the chambers of earlier megalithic tombs.

Early bronze age: a period in Britain from about 2200 BC during which first copper and then bronze were introduced.

Fengate ware: native late neolithic pottery, with large rims and small flat bases.

Food-vessel: heavy and squat flat-bottomed vessels of the early bronze age with moulded rims, profusely decorated with cord and impressed decoration.

Grooved Ware: formerly known as Rinyo-Clacton ware, this late neolithic ceramic style of flat-based, tub-shaped and bucket-shaped pots decorated in geometrical lines has often been associated with henges.

Henge: an approximately circular ritual earthwork of the late neolithic and early bronze age.

Megalithic: a monument constructed of large stones (*mega* = big, *lithos* = stone).

Megalithic tomb: a burial place such as a passage-tomb built of big stones.

Neolithic: the new stone age. Archaeologically it is divided in Britain into an **early** period from about 4500 to 3500 BC, with pioneering settlers living in farmsteads; a **middle** period, *c*.3500 to 2700 BC, with widening social contacts, expanding trade in stone axes, and settlement sites such as causewayed enclosures and defended villages; and a **late** period (*c*.2700 to 2200 BC), during which henges and stone circles developed.

Passage-tomb: a round megalithic tomb with a passage leading to a burial chamber, common in Ireland and Scotland.

Peterborough ware: native middle neolithic bowls, widespread in England, round-based, heavily rimmed and lavishly decorated with impressions of fingertips, bird bones or twigs.

Phallus: the male sexual organ.

Plateau: the interior of a henge.

Portals: upright stones or posts at the entrance to a henge.

Rusticated ware: pottery with roughened surfaces often made by fingertip pinching.

Wessex: the area of southern England including Wiltshire, Dorset, Berkshire, Somerset and Hampshire. It supported a large prehistoric population on its easily worked chalk soils.

10
Twenty sites to visit

Most henges are ploughed out and so inconspicuous that they repay a visit only by the most devoted of enthusiasts. The twenty described below are in better condition. Where a site is on private land, permission to see it should be obtained from the nearby farm. More details about them and their finds can be found in the guides and other books listed in chapter 11.

Arbor Low, Derbyshire. SK 160636. 13 km (8 miles) south-east of Buxton. A charge is made. A circle-henge (II). The stone circle is fallen. So is the central cove. There is a round barrow on the bank by the southern entrance. Gib Hill round barrow is just west of the henge.

Balfarg, Fife. NO 281032. 1.5 km (1 mile) north-west of Markinch. Free. This circle-henge (I) has been partly restored with posts marking the places where posts and stones once stood.

Ballymeanoch, Argyll, Strathclyde. NR 833963. 8 km (5 miles) north of Lochgilphead. Private. A small Class II henge which has a cairn inside it. The Kilmartin Stones stand just to the north-east.

Broomend of Crichie, Aberdeenshire, Grampian. NJ 779196. 1.5 km (1 mile) south of Inverurie. Private. A circle-henge (II) of which little survives of the stones of the circle or of the avenues that approached it. A Pictish carved stone has been added to the henge.

Cairnpapple, West Lothian. NS 987717. 1.5 km (1 mile) east-southeast of Torphichen. Charge. Although robbed, the places where stones stood in this circle-henge (II) are clearly marked. It is also possible to enter the later cairn inside the earthwork.

Castleruddery, County Wicklow. S 925937. 8 km (5 miles) north-east of Baltinglass. Free. A circle-henge (IC). Its east entrance is flanked by portal stones of white quartz.

Dowth Q, County Meath. O 034742. 3 km (2 miles) east of Slane. Private. An impressive henge (IIC). It is 500 metres north-east of the Dowth passage-tomb complex.

Giant's Ring, County Down. J 327677. 6 km (4 miles) south of Belfast. Free. An enormous Class IC or IIC henge 180 metres across. Near the centre is a megalithic tomb in which cremations were discovered.

Grange, County Limerick. R 640410. 19 km (12 miles) south-southeast of Limerick. Free. A neatly reconstructed circle-henge (IC) with a paved east entrance. It is at the west of the Lough Gur complex.

King Arthur's Round Table, Cumbria. NY 523284. 1.5 km (1 mile) south-east of Penrith. Free. A quite well preserved henge (II). A cremation trench was discovered at its centre. The henge is 400 metres east of the Mayburgh (IC) earthwork.

Knowlton, Dorset. SU 025100. 5 km (3 miles) south-west of Cranborne. Free. A henge (II) in fine condition with a ruined twelfth-century church inside it. A large but ploughed-down earthwork enclosure surrounds Knowlton Farm just to its south. 60 metres to the east is the Great Barrow.

Maumbury Rings, Dorset. SY 690899. On the southern outskirts of Dorchester. Free. A splendid henge (I) whose deep shafts were filled in when the site was converted into a Roman amphitheatre.

Mayburgh, Cumbria. NY 519285. 1.5 km (1 mile) south-east of Penrith. Free. An enormous henge (IC) with an eastern entrance and a gigantic stone-piled bank. A single standing stone near its centre is reputed to be the survivor of a small four-poster stone circle.

Muir of Ord, Ross and Cromarty, Highland. NH 527497. 13 km (8 miles) west-northwest of Inverness. On a golf course. Private. A small henge (II) with east-west entrances.

Ring of Brodgar, Orkney. HY 294134. 6 km (4 miles) north-east of Stromness. Free. A splendid circle-henge (II) with tall standing stones. There are north-west and south-east entrances but no sign today of the outer bank.

Stonehenge, Wiltshire. SU 123422. 3 km (2 miles) west of Amesbury. Charge. An earthwork transitional between the middle neolithic causewayed enclosures and the late neolithic henges. For guidance about positions note that the Heel Stone is at the north-east. South is at the narrow causeway across the ditch opposite the shortest stone of the outer circle. Concrete rings mark the positions of some Aubrey Holes inside the inner bank. The low outer bank can still be seen.

Stones of Stenness, Orkney. HY 306125. 6 km (4 miles) north-east of Stromness. Free. A fine circle-henge (I) just south of the Ring of Brodgar. Four stones survive of a possible twelve. A Scottish form of cove stands near the centre.

Stripple Stones, Cornwall. SX 144752. 11 km (7 miles) north-east of Bodmin. Private. The stones of this circle-henge (I) are toppled or removed and the central stone is prostrate. The site is about 69 metres across.

Thornborough, North Yorkshire. SE 285795. 1.5 km (1 mile) north-east of West Tanfield. Private. The three Class IIA henges lie in a 1.5 km long NNW-SSE line. Gypsum from a few kilometres down the river Ure covered their banks. The central henge was built over a middle neolithic cursus.

Woodhenge, Wiltshire. SU 150434. 1.5 km (1 mile) north of Amesbury. Free. The bank and ditch of this henge (I) are much reduced. There is a north-northeast entrance. Inside the earthwork the positions of the six rings of posts are marked by concrete pillars, their widths reproducing the diameters of the original timbers. The flint-covered grave is near the middle of the rings.

In addition, the circle-henge of the **Devil's Quoits** (II), Oxfordshire, SP 411048, is to be reconstructed. A reduced plan of **Goldington** henge (I), Bedfordshire, TL 079503, is marked out in front of the entrance of the Tesco supermarket that has been built on its site. There is a photographic display inside the store.

11
Further reading

Useful guidebooks
Dyer, J. *The Penguin Guide to Prehistoric England and Wales*. Penguin, 1981.
Dyer, J. *Discovering Prehistoric England*. Shire, 1993.
Evans, E. *Prehistoric and Early Christian Ireland*. Batsford, 1966.
Feacham, R. *Guide to Prehistoric Scotland*. Batsford, 1977.
Harbison, P. *Guide to the National Monuments in the Republic of Ireland*. Gill & Macmillan, 1970.
Hawkes, J. *The Shell Guide to British Archaeology*. Michael Joseph, 1986.
Houlder, C. *Wales: an Archaeological Guide*. Faber, 1974.
Thomas, N. *Guide to Prehistoric England*. Batsford, 1976.

Background reading
Burgess, C. *The Age of Stonehenge*. Dent, 1980.
Darvill, T. *Prehistoric Britain*. Batsford, 1987.
Dyer, J. *Ancient Britain*. Batsford, 1990.
Harbison, P. *Pre-Christian Ireland*. Thames & Hudson, 1988.
Mercer, R. J. *Causewayed Enclosures*. Shire, 1990.

Books on henges
Atkinson, R. J. C. *Stonehenge*. Pelican, 1979.
Atkinson, R. J. C.; Piggott, C. M.; and Sandars, N. K. *Excavations at Dorchester, Oxon*. Ashmolean Museum, Oxford, 1951.
Burl, A. *Prehistoric Avebury*. Yale University Press, 1979.
Burl, A. *The Stonehenge People*. Dent, 1987.
Castleden, R. *The Making of Stonehenge*. Routledge, 1993.
Cunnington, M. *Woodhenge*. Simpson, 1929.
Harding, A. F., with Lee, G. *Henge Monuments and Related Sites of Great Britain*. British Archaeological Reports 175, 1987.
Newham, C. A. *The Astronomical Significance of Stonehenge*. Blackburn, 1972.
Wainwright, G. *The Henge Monuments*. Thames & Hudson, 1989.

Important articles on henges
ApSimon, A., *et al.* 'Gorsey Bigbury, Cheddar, Somerset', *Proceedings of the Bristol University Spelaeological Society* 14 (2) (1976), 155-83.

Barclay, G. J. 'Sites of the Third Millennium BC to the First Millennium AD at North Mains, Strathallan, Perthshire', *Proceedings of the Society of Antiquaries of Scotland* 113 (1983), 122-281.

Barclay, G. J. 'Henge Monuments: Reappraisal or Reductionism?', *Proceedings of the Prehistoric Society* 55 (1989), 260-2.

Burl, A. 'Henges: Internal Features and Regional Groups', *Archaeological Journal* 126 (1969), 1-28.

Catherall, P. D. 'Henges in Perspective', *Archaeological Journal* 128 (1971), 148-53.

Catherall, P. D. 'Henge Monuments: Monument or Myth?', in C. Burgess and R. Miket, *Settlement and Economy in the Third and Second Millennia BC*. British Archaeological Reports, 1976, 1-9.

Clare, T. 'Towards a Reappraisal of Henge Monuments', *Proceedings of the Prehistoric Society* 52 (1986), 281-316.

Clare, T. 'Towards a Reappraisal of Henge Monuments: Origins, Evolutions and Hierarchies', *Proceedings of the Prehistoric Society* 53 (1987), 457-77.

Clark, J. G. D. 'The Timber Monument at Arminghall and Its Affinities', *Proceedings of the Prehistoric Society* 2 (1936), 1-51.

Pollard, J. 'Structured Deposition at Woodhenge', *Proceedings of the Prehistoric Society* 61 (1995), 137-56.

Stout, G. M. 'Embanked Enclosures of the Boyne Region', *Proceedings of the Royal Irish Academy* 91C (1991), 245-84.

Index

Page numbers in italic refer to illustrations.